THE CREATIVE SPARK

THE CREATIVE SPARK

Igniting Innovation in Every Aspect of Your Life

B. VINCENT

QuillQuest Publishers

CONTENTS

Chapter 1: Understanding Creativity

Characterizing Innovativeness: Exploring the Substance of Advancement

Innovativeness, often regarded as the foundation of growth, remains a signal that illuminates the paths to fresh arrangements, imaginative expressions, and earth-shattering breakthroughs. In this inaugural research, we go on a journey to untangle the perplexing concept of imagination, comprehending its multi-layered characteristics and enormous repercussions across several domains of human endeavor.

Moving beyond basic creative energy or logical inventiveness, we discover the essence of innovativeness as a unique combination of creative mind, creativity, and critical thinking skills. Drawing on insights from enlightening figures in the fields of craftsmanship, science, and business, we provide a complete framework that goes beyond conventional bounds, providing a deep understanding of inventiveness' breakthrough potential.

Through engrossing stories and fascinating research, we explore the maze of innovation, understanding its role as both an incentive and a product of human desire. From the pioneering works of Renaissance polymaths to the problematic developments of contemporary visionaries, we trace the transforming path of imagination, uncovering its enduring legacy in shaping the course of history.

As we embark on this journey of revelation, let us do so with open minds and energized hearts, ready to welcome the unfathomable potential consequences that lay at the intersection of creative mind and understanding. By pursuing understanding imagination, we enlighten both the paths to growth and the essence of being human.

Disseminating Fantasies and Confusions: Enlightening Bits of Insight into Invention

In order to understand imagination, we must first remove the veil of misinterpretation that often obscures its manifestation. Throughout history, delusions and deceptions have cloaked imagination in personalities, relegating it to the realm of innate talent or the elusive virtuoso. However, as we peel back the layers of misinformation, we find a more nuanced reality—one that encourages diversity of thought and the democratization of progress.

Join us as we deconstruct these dreams one step at a time, revealing the inherent ambiguity of notions that confine imagination to a select few endowed with incredible abilities. From the mythology of the lone genius to the misperception of easy motivation, we confront these misconceptions with observational evidence and compelling stories, illuminating the fact that creativity is competence developed by conscious effort and consistency.

Following our exposure, we embrace the lavishness of inventiveness's embroidered artwork, recognizing its general availability and limitless possibility for expression. We commend the democratization of advancement through the accounts of ordinary individuals who have questioned the opportunities to unleash their imaginative potential, encouraging readers to recover their organization in the inventive approach.

As we embark on this path of illumination, let us set aside the shackles of misinterpretation in favor of a more comprehensive picture of innovativeness—one that celebrates the diversity of human experience while also recognizing the inherent ingenuity that exists inside each of us. In dispersed dreams, we prepare for a more promising future in which development has no limitations.

The Innovative Approach: Exploring the Phases of Development

Within the maze of imagination is a structured journey, depicted by specific stages that lead the development of ideas from inception to recognition. In this section, we embark on a journey through the creative flow, outlining the stages of creation as they unfold through motivation, ideation, and implementation.

Our research begins with the source of inventiveness: motivation. We unravel the mysteries of motivation, tracing its origins to various sources—be it natural wonders, noteworthy human contacts, or fortunate events. Through fascinating testimonies and shrewd studies, we delve into the systems that spark the flash of originality, lighting the flames of the creative mind within.

Motivation leads to ideation, which is fertile ground for the seeds of innovation to grow and bloom. Here, we delve into the complexity of ideation, looking at strategies for creating and refining ideas ranging from brainstorming sessions to sidelong reasoning tasks. We engage readers to leash the innovative capability of their minds through viable models and involved effort, resulting in a mother lode of imaginable outcomes.

However, the journey of innovativeness is incomplete without the final stage: implementation. Trailblazers transform ideas into tangible results via unwavering drive and clear vision, overcoming obstacles and seizing opportunities along the way. Through contextual analyses and genuine models, we gain bits of knowledge about the craft of execution, understanding the laws that assist effective advancement efforts.

As we move through the innovative flow, let us embrace the tremendous exchange of motivation, ideation, and execution, viewing each stage as a critical component in the development hardware. To grasp the stages of imagination, we provide ourselves with the tools and experiences necessary to explore the complexities of the creative journey and unleash our full imaginative potential.

Developing an Imaginative Mentality: Fostering the Seeds of Development

At the heart of every inventive endeavor lies the fertile soil of mentality—a rich tapestry of convictions, mentalities, and points of view that determine our approach to progress. In this section, we go deeply into the development of an innovative mindset, revealing the fundamental laws that foster adaptability, versatility, and visionary reasoning.

Developing an imaginative mindset begins with a fundamental shift in perception—a recognition that creativity is not a gift bestowed upon a select few, but rather a skill that can be honed and refined through deliberate practice. Through thoughtful activities and clever prompts, we invite readers to confront restrictive convictions and adopt a development-oriented mindset that values and promotes trial and error.

The development of interest—a ravenous appetite for learning and a continual search for understanding—is critical to building an inventive mindset. By using interest as a compass, we embark on a journey of exploration and revelation, unearthing hidden connections and unveiling unique experiences that inspire growth.

Similarly important is the cultivation of adaptability—an unwavering commitment to perseverance even in the face of adversity. Through the stories of pioneers who overcame adversity and triumphed, we gain insight into the flexibility mindset, viewing tragedies as opportunities for growth and learning.

As we navigate the landscape of mental development, let us embrace the incredible power of belief—the idea that inside each of us resides the ability to improve, create, and motivate. When we cultivate an inventive mindset, we sow the seeds of growth, which blossom into arrangements, creations, and imaginative grand opuses that improve our overall environment.

Embracing Disappointment: The Pot of Innovation.

In the chronicles of development, disappointment is shown not as a sign of defeat, but rather as a pot from which imagination emerges more grounded, stronger, and boundlessly polished. In this section, we confront the all-encompassing disappointment, highlighting its enormous potential as a critical motivator for development, learning, and progress.

Embracing disappointment begins with a shift in perspective—a reevaluation of problems as stepping stones toward supremacy rather than insurmountable obstacles. We delve into the stories of luminaries who have accepted disappointment as a sidekick on their innovative journey, emerging from adversity with newly discovered knowledge and fortitude.

The establishment of a development outlook—faith in the intrinsic limit of progress and the flexibility to continue forward despite setbacks—is critical to disappointment. Through practical tasks and clever prompts, we help readers to reconsider disappointment as a natural part of the creative flow, encouraging them to extract significant illustrations from each stumble and go forward with renewed confidence.

Similarly important is the celebration of trial and error—a desire to push boundaries, question shows, and examine an unfamiliar region in the pursuit of development. Through the stories of trailblazers who pondered resisting the status quo, we discover the astonishing ability to use trial and error, viewing disappointment not as a burden but as a sign of brave research.

As we explore the domain of disappointment, let us embrace its perplexing nature—not as a sign of failure, but as a guide to probabilities. By accepting failure, we open the door to limitless imagination, strength, and progress, transforming challenges into springboards for growth and motivation.

Chapter 2: Unleashing Your Imagination

Taking Advantage of Interest: Creating the Flash of Request

A flare of interest—an insatiable thirst for knowledge, a dogged quest for comprehension—is at the heart of every creative endeavor. In this exploration of the basic rule of freeing your creative mind, we look at the revolutionary power of interest as a catalyst for sparking inventive reasoning.

Interest entices us to study the obscure, scrutinize the familiar, and seek answers beyond the scope of the performance. We illuminate the horde of ways that interest fills the creative flow, kindling the blazes of development inside, through captivating stories and provocative bits of knowledge.

From the leading minds of history's most prominent pioneers to the inquisitive spirits of ordinary travelers, we discover the profound impact of curiosity on human progression and disclosure. Through their tales, we gain insight into the art of addressing, the joy of exploration, and the limitless possibilities that arise when we ask, "Why?"

As we delve deeper into the realms of interest, let us embrace the soul of request that lays dormant inside each of us, ready to be stirred and unleashed on the material of imagination. By capitalizing on curiosity, we open the door to a universe of miracles, motivation, and perpetual chance, where the journey of revelation transcends all reasonable constraints.

Care and Innovativeness: Maintaining Presence for Enlivened Creation

In today's fast-paced world, the craft of care provides a safe haven—a place where imagination may grow amidst the chaos. In this exploration of the second guideline of freeing your creative mind, we look at the harmonious relationship between care and imagination, revealing how developing presence improves our aptitude for inspired invention.

Care encourages us to fully embrace the present moment —to secure our mindfulness in the present time and place, free of the interruptions of disappointments or future nerves. Through the act of caring, we learn how to quiet the brain's never-ending chatter, resulting in a large size that takes into account the emergence of fresh experiences and brilliant ideas.

We unravel the science behind care by drawing on ancient pondering customs and modern neuroscience, probing how practices such as contemplation, breathwork, and body awareness can revamp the cerebrum, fostering greater clarity, center, and imaginative flow. We invite readers to embark on their care journey through interactive activities and guided reflections, discovering the breakthrough force of presence firsthand.

As we cultivate care as a basis for creative expression, let us welcome each moment with loving mindfulness, realizing that the wellspring of drive lies within the depths of peace. By sustaining our presence, we open the door to a reservoir of creativity that flows endlessly from the depths of our being, enriching our lives and our surrounds.

Animating imagination through play: rediscovering the delight of investigation.

In the midst of the hustle and bustle of daily life, the soul of play coaxes—a euphoric invitation to rediscover the inexplicable magic of childhood and unleash our inventive potential. In this exploration of the third guideline for unlocking your creative mind, we look at the tremendous power of energy in stimulating imagination and fostering a sense of curiosity.

Energy illuminates the creative mind, inviting us to let go of the shackles of self-earnestness and embrace the freedom of unrestricted expression. From the perspective of play, we rekindle our sense of wonder, embarking on psyche and soul journeys that transcend the demands of logic and reason.

From the fun-loving act of spontaneity to wacky trial and error, we look into a variety of ways to infuse our lives with the soul of play. We encourage readers to take advantage of their innate sense of aliveness by engaging in intuitive exercises and imaginative prompts, freeing their creative minds and opening up new areas of possibility.

As we embrace the revolutionary force of play, let us abandon the delight of study in favor of the pure joy of imaginative expression. For there are no limits to what we may achieve in the jungle gym of our creative mind, and every second is an opportunity for revelation and joy.

Different Reasoning Methods: Extending Skylines with Inventive Investigation

Chasing development, diverse logic serves as a compass, guiding us beyond the show's boundaries and into unknown realms of believability. In this exploration of the fourth guideline of releasing your creative mind, we look at the remarkable power of various reasoning strategies, revealing how they create imaginative skylines and promote imaginative arrangements.

Different reasoning encourages us to study different points of view, welcome ambiguity, and participate in crazy thoughts without judgment. We soar above straight thought designs by using unique reasoning, opening ourselves up to a kaleidoscope of possible outcomes and uncovering concealed associations that lead to novel experiences.

From meetings to creating new ideas to mind-planning, we study a plethora of distinct reasoning techniques designed to ignite the creative spark within. We invite readers to investigate many routes about these tactics using logical models and certifiable implementations, discovering firsthand the liberating force of broad thinking.

As we welcome distinctive reasoning as the foundation of inventive exploration, let us celebrate the abundance of variation and the brilliance of unconventional ideas. For by deviating from the usually recognized path, we pave the way for progress, prepare for forward leaps that shake the boat and shape the course of history.

Imagination Activities: Setting out on an excursion of propelled disclosure.

Within the sphere of creativity lies a goldmine of activities and exercises—doors to unlock the vast reserves of creative minds within us. In this exploration of the fifth standard of freeing your creative mind, we embark on a journey of revelation, delving into practical techniques designed to animate imagination and ignite the flames of development.

Inventive techniques serve as impetuses for exploration, encouraging us to stretch our creative muscles, seek new routes for revolutionary ideas, and push the boundaries of what is possible. From writing prompts to creative projects, we study a diverse range of activities designed to awaken and enable people from all disciplines and skill levels.

Through active participation and experiential learning, we cultivate a fun-loving soul of curiosity and trial and error, relishing the thrill of disclosure as we explore the imagined scenario. These activities, whether through individual reflection or collaborative endeavors, provide a tangible means of freeing our brains and reinvigorating our most audacious ambitions.

As we immerse ourselves in these imaginative works, let us approach each moment with a sense of transparency and wonder, realizing that within the demonstration of creation lies the capacity to transform ourselves and our environment. For by accepting the voyage of pushed disclosure, we embark on a journey of self-discovery and progress, where each challenge becomes an open door and each second an invitation to make again.

Chapter 3: Overcoming Creative Blocks

Distinguishing Inventive Blocks: Identifying Obstacles to Advancement

Obstacles frequently appear in the unexpected dance of imagination, producing shadowed places on the path to growth. In this analysis of the basic guideline for overcoming creative blocks, we delve into the maze of challenges that choke new articulation, illuminating common obstacles, and their hidden sources.

Imaginative obstacles appear in bunch structures, such as self-uncertainty, compulsiveness, or a dogged search for con-gruity. Through critical meditation and honest assessment, we invite readers to identify the specific restrictions that hinder their imaginative flow, believing that awareness is the most crucial step toward freedom.

From the deadening grip of dread to the suffocating load of assumption, we show the solid foundations of innovative blocks, untangling the tangled ropes that bind us to idleness and stagnation. Through sympathetic exploration and shared encounters, we foster a sense of fortitude, assuring readers that they are not alone in their fights.

As we explore the landscape of innovative obstacles, let us see every impediment not as a roadblock, but as an opportunity for growth and transformation. For by detecting and accepting our limitations, we allow ourselves to climb above them, unleashing the full extent of our imaginative potential on the world.

Developing Versatility: Developing Fortitude Despite Misfortune.

In the cauldron of imagination, flexibility seems as a promising sign—an unwavering companion who guides us through the most hazy of storms and propels us toward the shores of development. In this exploration of the second level of overcoming creative obstacles, we delve into the art of developing strength and discovering strategies for fast recovering from creative challenges and disasters.

Flexibility is more than just the ability to endure and thrive in the midst of adversity. Through stories of triumph over adversity and adaptability, even in the face of failure, we are inspired by the brave souls of those who have faced the challenges of imaginative vulnerability and emerged stronger on the other side.

The act of self-care is fundamental to the development of versatility—supporting our physical, profound, and mental well-being to help us through the trials of the inventive journey. From care routines to self-empathy, we look into a variety of ways for replenishing our resources and boosting our internal power.

As we embrace flexibility as the cornerstone of creative versatility, let us recognize the strength that exists within each of us, waiting to be awakened and released onto the material of imagination. In growing flexibility, we face the challenges of imaginative vulnerability but emerge altered, encouraged, and ready to conquer new heights.

Overcoming Dread and Self-Uncertainty: Confronting the Shadows of Imaginative Articulation

Dread and self-question prowl as formidable foes in the realm of imagination, attempting to extinguish the blazes of drive and silence the voice of progress. In this exploration of the third rule of overcoming imaginative obstacles, we confront these shadows head on, dismantling the false grip they have on our innovative demeanor.

Dread, delivered into the world from the unknown and fueled by the apparition of disappointment, deadens us with its cold grip, providing steadiness despite innovative problems. Self-questioning, or mumbling unceasing inquiries and reactions, undermines our certainty and diminishes our identity worth. Through thoughtful prayer and empathetic self-reflection, we shine a light on these inward evil presences, remembering them as stumbling blocks to our imaginative potential.

Armed with awareness and understanding, we go on a journey of self-strengthening, reclaiming our creative power from the grip of fear and self-question. Through care rehearsals and mental rethinking methods, we establish flexibility in the face of vulnerability, paving the way for creative freedom and self-acceptance.

As we navigate the maze of dread and self-question, keep in mind that boldness is not the absence of worry, but the ability to act in spite of it. Standing up to our shadows reveals hidden sources of unity and fearlessness, enabling us to rise above our limitations and unleash the full extent of our imaginative potential on the world.

Breaking Schedule: Embracing Oddity and Investigation.

Schedule, while relaxing in its universality, can also become the silent adversary of imagination—a stagnant lake in which development struggles to thrive. In this exploration of the fourth standard of overcoming creative barriers, we will delve into the incredible power of breaking schedule, embracing curiosity, and going into an uncharted territory.

The schedule, with its predictable rhythms and natural examples, might soothe us into a state of unconcern, stifling our creative thoughts and harboring our artistic spirits. By breaking free from the constraints of a timetable, we open ourselves up to new interactions, new perspectives, and unanticipated sources of drive.

Through deliberate demonstrations of suddenness and investigation, we disrupt the monotony of our daily lives, imbuing our reality with a sense of experience and likelihood. From pursuing new side interests to confronting new objections, we see peculiarity as a catalyst for inventive repair and development.

As we break free from the constraints of scheduling, let us enjoy the exhilarating journey of exploration and revelation, believing that it is only by traveling outside our customary domains of familiarity that we truly develop and advance. By embracing peculiarity and unexpectedness, we welcome the dream of motivation to move freely through the pathways of our creative mind, kindling the sparks of imagination and development.

Looking for Motivation: Developing the Rich Grounds of Innovation.

Motivation continues to be a guiding light and an endless reservoir of potential on the path to inventive articulation. In this exploration of the fifth rule for overcoming creative obstacles, we embark on a journey to find inspiration, exploring the various sources and innovative power that reignite our creative fire.

Motivation, like a gentle breeze, whispers insider information to those who are eager to accept its offerings. From the majesty of nature to the insight of ancient literature, we study the vast patchwork of motivation that surrounds us, gleaning knowledge from the world's miracles and the depths of human experience.

Through thorough perception and purposeful contemplation, we cultivate an open mind that is sensitive to the unassuming subtleties and fortuitous moments that flash our inventive creative minds. Whether we immerse ourselves in human expression, engage with foreign communities, or spend time with close friends, we discover that motivation knows no bounds and may be found in the most unexpected places.

As we go on the journey of finding motivation, let us approach each moment with kindness and respect, knowing that the source of motivation contains the power to improve our lives and our creative endeavors. Looking for motivation opens the door to a universe of limitless possibilities, where sparks of imagination ignite flares of development and creative mind.

Chapter 4: Nurturing a Creative Environment

Creating Space for Inventiveness: Developing Fruitful Grounds of Advancement

Within the material of our environmental aspects lies the ability of creating a climate that encourages and stimulates imaginative expression. In this exploration of the primary criterion of fostering an imaginative atmosphere, we delve into the specialty of creating physical and mental places that serve as incubators for development.

The real environment where we work and live plays an important role in shaping our creative outcomes. By creating situations that stimulate the faculties and encourage research, we provide fertile ground for the seeds of imagination to grow. From bustling collaborative places to tranquil nature retreats, we look into several environments that boost motivation and foster inventive thinking.

Similarly important is the creation of a psychological

environment that fosters clarity, attention, and openness to novel ideas. Through care techniques, mindfulness, and purposeful reflection, we clean the psyche's muck and provide an expansive place for innovative nuggets of knowledge to emerge. By encouraging an attitude of curiosity and wonder, we transform even the most mundane tasks into opportunities for disclosure and growth.

As we go on the journey of creating room for imagination, let us approach each climate with purpose and love, realizing the importance it has on our inventive strategy and outcome. By creating settings that support and stir, we provide a fertile foundation for ideas to sprout, thrive, and bloom into astonishing breakthroughs that better our lives and our surrounds.

Encourage Joint Action: Developing the Aggregate Virtuoso

Cooperation remains the underpinning of development —an orchestra of diverse voices singing songs of creativity and understanding. In this research of the second standard of maintaining an imaginative climate, we look at the exceptional power of coordinated effort, demonstrating its numerous rewards in invigorating innovation and fostering the exchange of ideas.

Joint endeavor transcends the constraints of individual ability, allowing us to pool our resources, perspectives, and interactions in the pursuit of common goals. We increase our inventive potential by harnessing the cooperative energy of collective knowledge, opening up new options and pushing the bounds of innovation further than we could alone.

From brainstorming sessions to interdisciplinary collaborations, we look into the various sorts of collaboration that ignite creativity and catalyze progress. By cultivating a culture of trust, openness, and mutual respect, we establish a safe haven for trial and error and idea exchange, where each voice is heard and each commitment is valued.

As we embrace the tremendous energy of cooperation, let us recognize that development thrives not in disengagement, but rather in the fertile soil of collective effort. Encouraging cooperation taps into humanity's collective virtuosity, winding around a tapestry of evolution that transcends individual bounds and transforms our environment.

Embracing Variety: Addressing the Strength of Diverse Points of View

Variety, in all of its richness and complexity, remains a cornerstone of imaginative greatness—an embroidery fashioned from a plethora of extraordinary points of view, foundations, and experiences. In this exploration of the third guideline of maintaining an inventive climate, we look at the tremendous force of accepting diversity, recognizing its major impact on cultivating development and propelling aggregate development.

Variety enriches the imaginative picture by providing a variety of perspectives, challenging assumptions, and sparking erratic bits of knowledge. By embracing variety in all of its forms—whether social, mental, or experiential—we provide fertile ground for the cross-fertilization of ideas and the development of creative solutions to complex problems.

We examine sensible strategies for bridging the strength of shifted viewpoints, ranging from comprehensive dynamic cycles to various group arrangements. By creating a climate that values diversity and supports a culture of inclusion, we create space for marginalized voices to be heard and underrepresented points of view to thrive.

As we embrace the incredible power of diversity, let us recognize that progress thrives in environments where each voice is valued and every point of view is acknowledged. By accepting diversity, we not only expand our imagination and development, but we also foster a sense of belonging and strength that benefits all of us.

Empowering Hazard Taking: Establishing a Culture of Striking Investigation

Every cutting edge contains a component of chance—a leap into the unknown, a desire to challenge the status quo, and a commitment to accept vulnerability. In this exploration of the fourth rule of maintaining an inventive climate, we look at the tremendous potential of encouraging risk-taking and creating a culture that values trial and error and rigorous investigation.

Risk-taking is the impetus that propels us beyond the limitations of comfort and security, motivating us to test the boundaries of what is possible. By developing a culture that values risk-taking as an essential component of imagination, we create an environment in which development thrives and notable ideas blossom.

From fostering a culture of mental security to promoting determined risk-taking, we look into practical methods for creating a stable environment that encourages strong trial and error. We allow people to tackle problems and pursue aggressive goals with assurance and flexibility by reevaluating disappointment as a distinctive component of the innovative flow and highlighting the lessons learned from catastrophes.

As we embrace the incredible power of risk-taking, let us remember that genuine growth comes not from avoiding risks, but from considering venturing into unfamiliar territory. By encouraging risk-taking, we pave the path for a future in which imagination surpasses all logical boundaries and each difficulty becomes an opportunity for growth and disclosure.

Giving Criticism and Support: Promoting Growth and Greatness

Criticism and support serve as vital nourishment for the seeds of imagination, stimulating growth, power, and grandeur. In this exploration of the fifth rule of maintaining an inventive climate, we delve into the tremendous force of providing constructive criticism and unwavering assistance, resulting in a setting in which individuals thrive and progress grows.

Productive criticism provides invaluable experiences that drive continuous progress and development. We help people polish their ideas, improve their skills, and unleash their full creative potential by providing explicit, significant critique that highlights characteristics and areas for progress. We offer a place of shelter for vulnerability and development by fostering a culture of criticism that values straightforwardness, authenticity, and compassion, in which people feel empowered to tackle problems and pursue their imaginative ambitions with confidence.

Similarly important is the provision of steadfast assistance—a lifesaver for those in need during times of vulnerability and uncertainty. By providing encouragement, recognition, and mentorship, we foster a sense of belonging to a place and community that fosters creativity and adaptability. Through thoughtful gestures, sympathy, and certification, we confirm each person's fundamental worth and competence, fostering a culture of assistance that celebrates wins while welcoming problems as opportunities for growth.

As we embrace the incredible force of criticism and support, let us remember that the journey of imagination is not a single one, but rather a collective endeavor driven by the assistance and comfort of others. For by providing critique and support, we nurture the seeds of imagination, building a culture in which development thrives and individuals succeed.

Chapter 5: Applying Creativity in Everyday Life

Coordinating Imagination into Routine Undertakings: Lifting the Everyday through Advancement

Inside the needlework of our daily routines lies a material brimming with untapped potential—a space in which even the most mundane tasks may be transformed into opportunities for creative expression and development. In this exploration of the fundamental rule of applying imagination in everyday life, we delve into the specialty of incorporating creativity into routine tasks, elevating the ordinary to the extraordinary.

Routine errands, ranging from household chores to administrative duties, sometimes serve as fertile ground for inventive research. By approaching these projects with a fresh perspective and an open mind, we uncover previously hidden opportunities for growth and productivity. We rejuvenate natural routines by presenting fresh techniques, merging cheerful components, or using out-of-the-crate configurations, all while instilling a sense of wonder and zeal.

Through relevant models and active exercises, we enable readers to unleash their creative potential in everyday moments. From reimagining everyday tasks as innovative challenges to creating an outlook of interest and trial and error, we invite readers to go on a journey of disclosure, where even the most simple activities become opportunities for self-expression and growth.

As we add imagination into ordinary tasks, let us enjoy the joy of discovery and investigation, believing that progress surpasses all logical constraints and originality has no bounds. By incorporating imagination into the fabric of our daily routines, we open up a universe of limitless possibilities and enrich our reality with moments of motivation, enjoyment, and fulfillment.

Critical Thinking and Imaginative Reasoning: Releasing Resourcefulness in Difficult Situations

In the midst of life's hardships, imaginative reasoning emerges as a hopeful sign—a guiding light that illuminates the path ahead despite vulnerability and struggle. In this exploration of the second rule of using imagination in everyday life, we look at the incredible power of inventive critical thinking tactics, providing readers with the tools and perspective they need to overcome obstacles.

Inventive critical thinking elevates traditional techniques, encouraging us to think beyond the requirements of demonstrating and discovering unique solutions to challenging problems. We unleash our resourcefulness and open up new avenues for attaining our goals by embracing uncertainty, re-imagining problems as opportunities, and employing innovative reasoning.

We outline the viability of imaginative critical thinking techniques in a variety of circumstances, ranging from individual concerns to professional difficulties, using genuine models and contextual assessments. Whether through meetings to develop new ideas, planning thinking philosophies, or parallel reasoning activities, we empower readers to harness their creative potential and approach problems with clarity and flexibility.

As we go on the journey of critical thinking with imaginative reasoning, let us embrace the spirit of trial and error and adaptability, understanding that each difficulty is an opportunity to grow and evolve. For, by unleashing our resourcefulness in the face of adversity, we overcome obstacles and pave the way for a more magnificent, more innovative future in which development thrives and flexibility reigns.

Developing Imaginative Propensities: Nurturing the Seeds of Invention

At the heart of every innovative endeavor is the cultivation of habits—ceremonies and timetables that serve as the soil in which creativity grows and twists. In this exploration of the third standard of applying imagination in daily life, we delve into the skill of cultivating innovative proclivities and allowing the seeds of imagination to bloom in every aspect of our lives.

Imaginative propensities are the foundation of imaginative greatness, affecting our thoughts, behaviors, and discernments in ways that promote growth and creativity. From practicing care and embracing trial and error to fostering a culture of deep-rooted learning and reflection, we look into a variety of factors that promote innovation and development.

We transform inventiveness from an erratic event into a lifestyle—a characteristic expansion of our being that combines each second with a flash of inspiration—thanks to the influence of trained instinct. By purposefully cultivating propensities for interest, strength, and receptiveness, we create a fertile field for invention and upward leaps.

As we embark on the journey of cultivating inventive propensities, let us approach each day with purpose and reason, believing that small, incremental adjustments can lead to substantial changes. By nurturing the seeds of imagination through creative proclivities, we pave the path for a universe of limitless possibility and an infinitely creative mind, where every second becomes an opportunity for driven articulation and development.

Imagination in Correspondence: Developing Stories and Associations

Correspondence is the foundation of human collaboration, built from strings of words, symbols, and emotions. In this exploration of the fourth standard of using imagination in everyday life, we delve into the craft of innovativeness in communication, looking at how narrative and imaginative articulation can create new associations and elicit good change.

Inventiveness imbues our correspondence with urgency and reverberation, transforming everyday exchanges into snapshots of association and drive. We create stories that have a big and profound impact on people by combining the power of narration, illustration, and symbolism, fostering compassion, understanding, and shared importance.

We create room for other points of view and interactions to be heard and considered by paying undivided attention and communicating compassionately. By embracing authenticity and frailty, we invite others into our lives, creating duties of trust and mutual esteem that transcend differences and unite us in the same way that humanity does.

As we confront the incredible energy of creativity in letters, let us recognize that each partnership represents an opportunity to stir, uplift, and involve others. We foster a culture of sympathy, empathy, and understanding by crafting stories and associations that touch the heart and stir the soul, transforming correspondence into a vehicle for good transformation and collective development.

Finding Happiness in Imaginative Pursuits: Creating a Life of Direction and Satisfaction

In the midst of the hustle and bustle of modern living, imaginative hobbies provide a safe haven—a place where we can escape the demands of everyday life and reconnect with our true selves. In this exploration of the fifth rule of applying imagination in daily life, we look at the game-changing impact of finding euphoria in creative endeavors and establishing a day-to-day existence rich with rationale, energy, and satisfaction.

Imaginative hobbies nourish the spirit, providing a channel for self-discovery, expression, and growth. Whether via painting, writing, music, or other creative endeavors, we tap into the sources of inspiration that are within us, releasing our creativity and experiencing glimpses of flow and brilliance.

Past basic enjoyment and inventive ambitions provide a major sense of direction—a calling that entices us to pursue our most profound interests and share our unique abilities with the world. By participating in exercises that align with our traits and aims, we infuse our lives with meaning and satisfaction, seeking bliss in the exhibition of creation itself.

As we embrace the revolutionary energy of finding bliss in imaginative pursuits, let us recognize that creativity knows no bounds and that every second is an opportunity for self-expression and research. For by cultivating a daily life rich in reason and satisfaction, we open the door to a universe of boundless opportunity and imagination, where each goal becomes a source of delight and inspiration.

Conclusion:

Recap of Key Bits of Knowledge: Embracing Innovative Excursions

As we conclude our inquiry into kindling imagination in all aspects of life, it is vital to consider the key pieces of knowledge and principles that have emerged throughout our journey. From comprehending the concept of creativity to creating an environment conducive to innovation, each section has provided critical perspectives and practical methods for unleashing our creative potential.

We began by delving into the essence of ingenuity, remembering it as a fundamental component of human communication and critical thinking. Through the examination of curiosity, caring, and liveliness, we discovered the incredible power of leveraging our inherent innovativeness and enjoying the joy of investigation.

Then we looked into the obstacles that regularly stymied our innovative expression, ranging from dread and self-uncertainty to the demands of regularity and familiarity. By confronting these obstacles and developing flexibility, we discovered how to approach challenges with courage and resolve, becoming more grounded and stronger in the process.

Throughout our journey, we emphasized the need of cultivating a stable climate that fosters innovation and development. We create room for imagination and people to thrive by accepting diversity, empowering risk-taking, and providing input and support.

As we reflect on these crucial pieces of information, let us carry forward the illustrations learned and continue to embrace the imaginative journey with open hearts and psyches. For every second is an opportunity for motivation, disclosure, and progress, and it is through our responsibility to the imagination that we improve our lives and have a big impact on our surrounds.

Reflection on Self-Awareness: Nurturing the Seeds of Potential

As we read through the pages of this book, we are compelled to embark on our own personal journey of growth and self-disclosure. Take a minute to reflect on the information you've learned and the changes you've seen along the way. Consider how your perspective on inventiveness has evolved and how you've implemented newly acquired facts in your own life.

Perhaps you've discovered hidden talents or regained a feeling of purpose in your creative pursuit. Perhaps you've confronted long-held concerns and uncertainties, emerging with a newfound sense of power and confidence in your abilities. In any case, recognize and celebrate the progress you've achieved on your creative journey thus far.

Remember that self-improvement is an ongoing cycle—an expedition rather than a goal. As you continue to develop your creativity, view each new test as an opportunity for learning and growth. Remain curious, open to new experiences, and kind with yourself as you explore the intriguing bends in the road of the inventive way.

By nurturing the seeds of possibility within yourself, you improve your own life and contribute to the collective woven artwork of human creativity. Your unique perspective, gifts, and dedication can have a big impact on others and the globe. Embrace the journey of self-awareness with courage and conviction, knowing that your creativity can have an impact.

Obligation to Activity: Embracing Innovation as a Lifestyle.

As we approach the completion of our investigation, let us restate our commitment to action—to incorporating the standards and knowledge gained from this journey into our daily routines. Imagination is more than simply a concept to be admired from a distance; it is a way of life to be truly embraced.

Pause for a moment to examine how you may incorporate creativity into your daily routines, collaborations, and passions. Recognize significant advances you can make to develop imagination in every aspect of your life, whether it's creating opportunities for imaginative leisure activities, approaching problems from a new perspective, or encouraging a development culture in your workplace or community.

Remember that minor efforts can cause significant effects. Accept every open door as an opportunity to experiment, learn, and grow. Step outside of your comfort zone, face obstacles, and accept failure as a necessary part of the creative process.

Resolving to engage in action and embrace imagination as a lifestyle improves your reality while also contributing to a more dynamic, innovative, and humane planet. Allow your creativity to serve as a source of inspiration, guiding you toward a future full of unlimited possibilities and potential.

Embracing Persistent Learning: A Deep-Rooted Exploration of Investigation

Our inquiry into innovativeness is not a goal, but rather an excursion—a journey of continuous learning, development, and growth. As we conclude our time together, let us embrace the idea that learning is a lifelong journey and that every second provides an opportunity for revelation and extension.

Maintain a curious and attentive attitude, eager to learn about new ideas, perspectives, and experiences. Develop a thirst for knowledge and a desire for growth that will propel you forward on your innovative journey. Search our teachers, associates, and networks of like-minded individuals who can support and guide you along the way.

Remember that creativity knows no bounds, and that there are always new frontiers to explore. You sincerely commit to investing resources in your development and advancement as an inventive person, whether by reading, visiting studios, or engaging in involved trial and error.

By accepting ongoing learning, you not only broaden your interpretation of the inventive method, but you also enrich your life with meaning, rationale, and satisfaction. Allow each new disclosure to feed your creativity and propel you to ever-higher heights of progress and self-expression.

Welcome to Join the Innovative People Group: Building Associations and Rousing Change.

As we get to the end of our journey, I'd want to welcome you to a vibrant and strong community of creative individuals who share your desire for growth and self-expression.

Together, we can continue to push and inspire one another, developing an imaginative and collaborative culture that extends far beyond the pages of this book.

Look for fantastic opportunities to connect with individual creatives who can offer aid, consolation, and valuable insights, whether through online meetings, neighborhood meetups, or innovative studios. Share your interactions, battles, and victories, and be open to learning from the varied perspectives and experiences of others.

Through our creativity and development, we can all make a positive difference in the world. Allow us to harness our community's collective energy and innovation to tackle complex problems, generate meaningful discussions, and inspire others to embrace their creative potential.

By banding together with people who share our values, we can amplify our impact and create a ripple effect of positive change that spreads throughout the world. Let us work together to create a future in which innovation is recognized, promoted, and valued as an essential component of being human.